Porters' rest, Piccadilly, London. The explanatory plate reads: 'On the suggestion of R. A. Slaney Esq., who for 26 years represented Shrewsbury in Parliament, this porter's rest was erected in 1861 by the vestry of St George Hanover Square, for the benefit of porters and others carrying burdens. As a relic of a past period in London's history, it is hoped that the people will aid in its preservation.'

STREET FURNITURE

Henry Aaron

Illustrated by Ian Sherren

Shire Publications Ltd

CONTENTS

 First published 1980. Second edition 1987; reprinted 1991. Shire Album 47. ISBN 0 85263 864 7.

Set in 9 point Times Roman and printed in Great Britain by C. I. Thomas & Sons (Haverfordwest) Ltd, Press Buildings, Merlins Bridge, Haverfordwest, Dyfed.

British Library Cataloguing in Publication Data available.

COVER: *Three-mantle gas lamp, Guildhall Yard, City of London.*

BELOW: *Signpost pointing to the hamlet of Come to Good, near Truro, Cornwall.*

Rare rustic-style seat, Hendon, North-west London.

INTRODUCTION

The passage of nearly two thousand years separates the setting up of Romano-British milestones from the present-day surveillance of traffic by closed-circuit television. At first glance there might seem little connection between the two but they have both served a common purpose of helping the traveller. Such objects erected on or adjacent to the public highway have come to be known as street furniture, a generic term embracing a vast array of past and present accessories intended to cater for road users.

The design, positioning and purpose of much of the street furniture we see today has been influenced by the needs of traffic and the needs created by traffic. The nature and volume of this traffic has changed dramatically over the years and an absorbing aspect of street furniture is its reflection of contemporary life and ways of getting about, be it on foot, by horse, electric tram or the internal combustion engine.

Street furniture comprises everyday things which are taken for granted by some people and do not arouse a curiosity rewarded by interesting facets of social history and pleasures of elegant design. Sadly, too, street furniture has become a target for widespread damage and destruction not only by senseless individuals but also, at times, by local authorities and developers.

However, there is a healthy interest in different kinds of furniture by those with eyes to see. Old lamp posts have been saved either singly or in quantity for many years and superannuated gas lamps now adorn numerous front gardens up and down Britain. Admittedly their new owners have sometimes had the posts painted in rebellious colours but at least they are helping to preserve genuine originals rather than latter-day imitations which are abhorrent to the purist.

Old letter boxes have also been put to practical use by those fortunate enough to possess them and there even exists a society dedicated to the study of letter boxes and their history. Similarly, coal plates attract their devotees who are not averse to getting down on hands and knees to take rubbings of worthy examples. Despite, or perhaps because of, extensive depredations in their respective fields, cast iron and wrought iron draw enthusiastic followings whilst the older types of bollard provide a specialised subject meriting examination. Where such activities foster awareness they are to be encouraged. Where awareness fosters careful documentation or preservation it is to be commended.

LEFT: *An isolated Romano-British milestone standing near the fort of Vindolanda, Northumberland. Regrettably there is now no trace to be seen of any inscription.*

RIGHT: *One of a series of milestones beside the A30 road between Salisbury and Shaftesbury. Some milestones are distinguished for the peculiar ways in which they display place-names. This one is representative in its use of the old forms of 'Sarum' and 'Shaston'.*

MILESTONES AND MILEPOSTS

The erection of milestones and mileposts perfectly illustrates the association between the proliferation of certain kinds of street furniture and particular eras in history, in this case the Roman occupation and the advent of the turnpike trusts.

An attendant feature of the Roman road was the Roman milestone. The word mile is derived from *mille passus,* indicating a thousand paces of approximately 58 inches (1473 mm) each. Hence it follows that a Roman mile was about two-thirds of a furlong (135 m) shorter than the present English mile, which was not defined by statute as being 5280 feet (1609 m) until 1593.

Though Romano-British roads formed a very extensive network, less than a hundred milestones of the period have been authoritatively identified. As the winning and dressing of building stone can be an arduous business it seems probable that milestones were removed for other uses after the Roman withdrawal in AD 407. Less forgivable is a lack of concern for archaeological matters which has allowed known stones to become lost in more recent times.

The comparative dearth of Romano-British milestones means that there are now few to be seen in situ or in museums. Small concentrations have been found in Cumbria and South Wales, and the British Museum (London), the National Museum of Wales (Cardiff) and the Chesters Museum (Northumberland), amongst others, possess examples from various places.

The Romano-British milestone was not standardised in its shape or size and ranged from the small rough block of stone to the well dressed cylinder standing perhaps 5 feet (1.5 m) above ground level. Of necessity inscriptions were rather more regular and, in addition to the mileage, sometimes included the prefix MP standing for *mille passus* (singular) or *milia passuum* (plural), the letter A denoting 'from', the name of the settlement whence the measurement was taken, and a dedication in honour of a particular emperor or consul.

Turnpike trusts lasted from early in the eighteenth century until the latter part of the nineteenth century, by which time the majority of toll roads had become free. It was incumbent upon trusts to set up sign-posts and mileage markers and this has resulted in a fine legacy of diverse styles of stones and iron posts, in some instances peculiar to quite short lengths of road.

Besides the requisite mileages the name of at least one place on the route was generally shown, sometimes in abbreviated and puzzling form. There might also be complementary arrows or fingers pointing in the appropriate direction. Furthermore, many milestones, being relatively little moved objects, have been incised with the arrow-like bench mark of the Ordnance Survey. Whilst much of the lettering on milestones is simple or crude, some was beautifully executed although a large proportion of the population was then unable to read. Additional or alternative embellishments were not unusual and markers beside the A22 and B1368 roads may be cited respectively for their display of the Pelham buckle and Bow bells and of the arms of Trinity Hall College, Cambridge.

LEFT: *A slightly dilapidated, but nonetheless interesting, milepost beside the A619 road near Baslow, Derbyshire. The cast place-name 'London' allows the post to be used virtually anywhere in Britain. Appropriate local place-names and distances are painted on the panels below as required.*

RIGHT: *An iron milepost beside the A6105 road near Duns, Scotland. The head of the post is of a style much used in the Borders region and Northumberland but the posts themselves vary in height and may be fluted or plain.*

One of a pair of granite horse-blocks in Waterloo Place, Westminster. The inscription reads: 'This horse-block was erected by desire of the Duke of Wellington, 1830.'

CATERING FOR HORSE TRAFFIC

For long before motor vehicles invaded the roads of Britain the horse reigned supreme as a means of transport. This primacy of the horse brought about street furniture that might be crudely described as being of a 'give and take' nature.

Getting on or off a horse is not always an easy or elegant operation and mounting blocks of brick or stone were put up to help riders mount and dismount. Many such blocks occur on private property and therefore do not qualify as street furniture but for good examples of those that remain beside the public highway the most likely places include outside old churchyards and inns.

Although horses were once used in very large numbers, both for riding and for draught, the way in which some were treated by their employers was not altogether kind and generous. In 1859 the Metropolitan Free Drinking Fountain Association (later renamed the Metropolitan Drinking Fountain and Cattle Trough Association) was founded to provide fountains of healthy drinking water for the populace. Within a few years a concern for animal welfare prompted that commendable body to set up water troughs at the roadside for free use by driven animals. In all the Association has been responsible for, or a party to, the positioning of nearly one thousand troughs in Britain and overseas and of this total about half were located in the London area. Early troughs were of wood or iron but have been superseded by the more familiar ones of granite comprising a deep trough set above a shallower dog trough at about road level. Many of these troughs still survive in situ though generally they are no longer replete with water.

With the advances made in street cleaning by mechanical means the street orderly is becoming almost extinct. In their heyday an army of street orderlies was responsible for sweeping the streets and pavements, removing horse droppings and spreading grit or sand when necessary. To assist them in these duties orderlies were equipped with a barrow, broom and shovel, augmented by bins placed at judicious intervals along the pavement.

One of the principal functions of the bins was to hold grit or sand for spreading on the roads if they became slippery for horses. A hinged or sliding lid at the top of the bin allowed for the bulk supply of grit or sand, which could be shovelled out through a hole at pavement level as required. A further use of some bins was to act as temporary holders of swept-up rubbish. Wire baskets might also be attached to the outside of a bin to take litter from passers-by.

Street bins were normally constructed of cast iron and they often bore the name of the local authority or such appellations as 'Street Orderly Bin', 'Grit Bin' or 'Sand Bin'. Spikes along the ridge served as both a decorative feature and a deterrent to those tempted to sit on the top. An alternative form of bin was fabricated, often in semicircular shape, from sheet and angle iron. Being of somewhat lighter construction than the cast type, these bins tended to deteriorate more quickly and are now comparatively rare.

A fine example of a mounting block in the village of Bradwell-on-Sea, Essex. Note the iron post, which may be unique.

ABOVE: *One of the three ranges of tethering posts beside the A6 road in Market Harborough, Leicestershire.*

BELOW: *An extra large granite MDF&CTA cattle trough in Clapham, South London. Whether or not replete with water, cattle troughs tended to collect a certain amount of litter. Now that the majority of troughs are dry some local authorities have taken to using them as flower beds.*

LEFT: *An aged cannon put to use as a pavement post in Southwark, South London. Slight traces may still be seen of the original mountings.*

RIGHT: *One of several similar bollards in Northampton.*

BOLLARDS

To the present-day motorist a bollard is either a modern concrete post at the road-side or an internally illuminated metal box standing on a traffic island or roundabout. Although their appearance and function have altered in the twentieth century much use has been made of bollards since the eighteenth century.

In the past bollards were set up to prevent, or at least discourage, encroachment of vehicles on to the pavement and around the end of the eighteenth century their erection received impetus from the formation of paving commissions, whose task it was to improve the lot of pedestrians by the provision and protection of pavements and kindred facilities. Bollards were also used to prevent horse-drawn vehicles, and later lorries and vans, from coming into contact with the sides of entrances and with buildings close to the street.

Early posts were of wood but in due course it became obvious that iron was a material better suited to withstand the ravages of careless driving and increasingly heavy vehicles. To some extent redundant cannon were with but slight modification put to good use as pavement posts though by far the most were made specifically for the job, either in the semblance of old cannon complete with a half ball protruding from the muzzle or in alternative and more ornate forms.

On the grounds of antiquity alone gun posts are of interest and with a little experience it is not very difficult to distinguish the genuine from the false – shape, finish and the presence of trunnions being clues that betray one or the other. However, bollards made to look something like cannon are no less interesting than those which inspired them. After all, the two types were often employed more or less contemporaneously, which is more than can be said of recent copies of old gas lamps.

Many bollards are easy to date within reasonably narrow limits because they bear a royal cipher or because a particular year has been cast around the outside of the barrel. The names of parishes and commissions, an assortment of shapes and some degree of decoration add to the attractions of bollard hunting. On the other hand the names of the ironfounders who made early bollards are frequently non-evident or absent and may, perhaps, be established only by searching through old catalogues and other records where these are still extant.

London is undoubtedly a bollard hunter's paradise as posts of various ages and types stand in many parts of the metropolis. Hunters outside London are less fortunate because posts in the provinces do not occur in such concentrations but perseverance may well be rewarded by the discovery of rare, if not unique, examples. For the connoisseur places worth exploring include Birmingham, Buxton and Portsmouth.

LEFT: *One of a group of similar bollards in Cheltenham, Gloucestershire. Although this bollard and the one in Northampton illustrated on page 9 exemplify the move away from mock cannon forms it will be noticed that the semblance of a surmounting cannonball has not been entirely dispensed with.*

RIGHT: *Although dated 1864, this bollard in Buxton, Derbyshire, displays a complete divergence from earlier cannon forms.*

LEFT: *Twin-spouted pump in the village of Preston Candover, Hampshire.*

RIGHT: *This pump standing beside the A4 near Thatcham, Berkshire, is one of several survivors from a series set up in the 1750s to provide water to help lay the dust on the road between London and Bath.*

PUMPS AND STANDPIPES

Now that water can be easily obtained in the home at the turn of a tap the hardships that confronted consumers in the past tend to be forgotten. Not until the twentieth century did most urban households in Britain have piped water and even now numerous remote farms and homesteads are dependent upon natural sources.

In former times those who were not fortunate enough to have a piped supply or to possess a pump or well of their own were obliged to make use of a public source of supply, which was not necessarily close at hand. Such points of supply, which included conduits and fountains, wells, pumps and standpipes, were often few and far between and the purity of the water itself was sometimes questionable. Many of these sources survive in public places but not all are still in working order. Where villages retain a standpipe or two it will very frequently be found that they were made by Glenfield and Kennedy of Kilmarnock, who were suppliers of standpipes and drinking fountains throughout Britain.

Before the industrial revolution pumps were locally manufactured and had more individuality than those subsequently produced in quantity. Early pumps tended to be of rudimentary construction, perhaps being simply boxed in with wood and lacking in much ornamentation. Nor were their lead pipes and spouts conducive to good health. With the increasing use of cast iron, pumps became more elaborate in appearance. Decoration ranged from the attractive to the indifferent. Much the same might be said of the shelters put up over village pumps, which varied from the severely utilitarian to the painfully pretentious. There were also hybrid types of pump in which the pump was combined with a street light, a union rather unattractive in Hemel Hempstead and executed far more pleasantly in Southwold.

Not all roadside pumps were intended for only domestic purposes. Some also supplied animal drinking troughs and some were used for filling water carts and thirsty traction engines. The widespread use of traction engines for agriculture and general haulage lasted from about 1870 to 1920 and the larger pumps, occasionally with two spouts, may date from this period.

Another application was served by the pumps erected in the middle of the eighteenth century alongside what is now the A4 road. Spaced at approximately 2 mile (3 km) intervals, these pumps were set up specifically to provide water for laying the dust on the busy road between London and Bath in stagecoach days. A number of the pumps still stand but in varying stages of decay, as is not surprising in view of their age.

LEFT: *A pretentious canopy over a green-painted but otherwise commonplace Glenfield and Kennedy standpipe in Nenthead, Cumbria.*

RIGHT: *This simple but practical standpipe in Aveton Gifford, Devon, contrasts strongly with the previous example.*

LEFT: *A 12-inch (305 mm) diameter coal plate by Hayward Brothers of Borough, South London, one of several large-scale suppliers in the nineteenth century.*

RIGHT: *Cover to a Gas Light and Coke Company gas supply valve. The GL&CC, formerly the Chartered Gas Light and Coke Company, was the world's first gas-producing company, having been founded in 1812. Covers bearing the initials GLCC are therefore amongst the oldest to be found.*

HOLE COVERS AND INDICATORS

Electricity, gas, oil, telephones and water are collectively referred to as 'services', and coal will be considered with these for the purposes of this chapter. At one time or another each of the six has reached the consumer by underground ways requiring access from pavement or road. Such access points have given rise to a large and very varied range of hole covers which deserve examination by the street furniture enthusiast.

In past centuries town houses were often built in terraces and with underground cellars for coal, then relatively cheap, plentiful and virtually the only means of heating. Terraced construction restricted the manner in which fuel could be delivered but one solution was to provide a hole in the pavement so that coal might be shot straight into the store below. For the safety of pedestrians it was necessary that every coal hole had its covering plate and in recent years these have become a subject for specialist study.

Coal plates are usually circular and between 12 and 24 inches (305-610 mm) in diameter, some embodying a number of glass ports to admit a little light into the cellar. Unlike much cast iron work, they frequently exhibit the name and sometimes the address of their makers and these details can hold valuable clues for students of industrial history.

Although not found in such concentrated variety and perhaps not as attractive as coal plates, other hole covers should not be overlooked. The covers to electricity, gas and water mains are not without merit and a collection of surface patterns might be made by taking rubbings, or a record of manufacturers' names and addresses could be built up. Some covers still bear the initials or names of former undertakings dating from long before nationalisation and are worthy of note in consequence.

All five services have their own service indicator posts. These are posts at the roadside which carry plates indicating the presence of or access to an underground cable or pipe. Basic information may include the type of service or facility, the size of cable or pipe, its depth and its perpendicular and lateral distances from the post.

In common with milestones and signposts some service indicator posts were defaced or removed just before or during the Second World War in case they might have proved useful to the enemy in the event of an invasion.

There used to be considerable differences in plates from one undertaking or county to another but nowadays posts have been or are being replaced by modern concrete or metal ones and old indicators with screw-on or slot-in numbers are disappearing as a result.

A hitherto somewhat neglected field therefore calls for urgent attention before more old-style plates and posts become redundant and are lost forever.

ABOVE: *Iron and concrete cover to a Post Office cable jointing pit. Some of these covers bear the inscription 'Post Office Telegraphs' and not the more common 'Post Office Telephones'.*

BELOW LEFT: *An Act of Parliament passed in 1707 called for the setting up of indicators to mark the proximity of stopcocks for fire-fighting purposes. Fire hydrant indicators are therefore one of the oldest types of indicator. Although indicators are being standardised many different shapes and sizes remain in use. This wall plate of about 1900 in Yeovil, Somerset, clearly shows the distance of the hydrant.*

BELOW RIGHT: *An iron fire hydrant indicator post of a rare type in Hatfield Peverel, Essex.*

LEFT: *A late nineteenth-century gas lamp in Dartmouth, Devon, discreetly converted to electricity.*

RIGHT: *An awe-inspiring multicoloured lantern in Milford, Surrey. Note the occupational pestle and mortar surmounting the ventilator.*

GAS LAMPS

Pall Mall, Westminster, was the first public thoroughfare in Britain to be lit by a series of gas lamps on free-standing posts. This came about in 1807 as a result of the efforts of F. A. Winzer, who was also instrumental in founding the Chartered Gas Light and Coke Company in 1812 and thus pioneered the gas-producing industry.

Despite the improvement upon what had been known previously, the amount of illumination afforded by early gas lamps was very meagre, especially when compared with the output of today's street lights. The burners frequently consisted of nothing more sophisticated than a metal fishtail giving a poor yellow light. Not before the introduction of mantles in 1885 did the standard improve. In its best known form the mantle consisted of a dome of cotton netting impregnated with salts which made for a whiter and far more brilliant light. The use of curved reflectors also helped to make the most of the available light.

Though poor by present standards, the Pall Mall lamps were effective enough to herald the proliferation of gas lamps in large towns all over Britain. An increasing demand for gas led to the building or enlarging of private and municipal gasworks supplying street lamps as well as homes and factories. The gas industry ramified to such an extent that at the time of nationalisation in 1949 more than a thousand separate undertakings were absorbed by the newly formed gas boards.

Until street lamps could be automatically lit and extinguished it was necessary for lamplighters to work their way round the streets at dusk and dawn. Armed with long poles, they would poke a lever or pull at a ring on a chain to put on or off each lamp in turn.

Passed by many thousands of people and probably noticed by few, this magnificent three-lamp standard stands amongst a welter of old and not so old street furniture in Trafalgar Square, Westminster.

In their Victorian and Edwardian heyday the range of designs in cast iron posts was prodigious, whilst the lanterns appeared in many shapes and sizes including four-, six- and eight-paned and globular specimens. Early posts were often not very tall and as stone throwing was not unknown the glass panes were frequently smashed. With the very much taller columns of today this pastime seems to have all but disappeared. In some instances panes were coloured blue, red or white and bore, perhaps, either the street name, the word 'Danger', an indication of a nearby fire station or brief details of a business outside which the lamp stood. Sadly, such interesting lamps are now very few and far between.

Further variety in the appearance of posts was provided by different types of ventilator, which might take the form of a slightly squashed top hat or a discreet finial, and by different styles of ladder rest. Ornamentation was sometimes taken to great lengths and included cherubs, fishes, mythical creatures, foliage and so on. In Scotland, particularly, crowns adorn the tops of many lanterns.

Although rudimentary in appearance, the decoration on this pair of lamps in Peebles, Borders, follows the Scottish practice of having lanterns surmounted with crowns.

One of the crown-surmounted letter boxes peculiar to Liverpool. This box was made by Cochrane and Company of Dudley and dates from 1863. Oddly and dangerously, it faces the road.

LEFT: *A 'lamp box' attached to a telegraph pole in Lowick, Northumberland. This box was made by W. T. Allen and Company of London and dates from the reign of George VI.*

RIGHT: *A double-aperture letter box in Holborn, London. This box appears to have been made by Andrew Handyside and Company of Derby and dates from the reign of Edward VII.*

LETTER BOXES

The first roadside pillar boxes in the British Isles were four boxes brought into use in St Helier, Jersey, in 1852. These boxes were successful and others were introduced on the mainland the following year, but pillar boxes had been in use on the Continent for some time before 1852. That Britain had pillar boxes at all is attributable to the recommendation of Anthony Trollope, the author, who was also a Post Office surveyor for several years during the reign of Queen Victoria.

Since their inception it has been customary for most letter boxes to carry a royal cipher. This may be of assistance in dating a box within limits but it should be borne in mind that whereas the monogram of the reigning monarch is normally applied to boxes when they are new the ciphers on some, but not all, old boxes have since been updated, as witness boxes which patently date from before 1952 but currently bear the initials of Elizabeth II. Although the reign of Edward VIII was short a goodly number of boxes bearing his monogram still exist, notably in Glasgow and London.

In addition to ciphers, other accretions of interest include stamp vending machines, first introduced in 1884, and the oval signs occasionally attached to the tops of boxes to indicate the direction of a nearby post office.

Whilst letter boxes are now commonly painted red, pillar boxes painted blue and meant for the posting of air letters only were used for a brief period in the 1930s.

There are approximately one hundred thousand boxes of various types in use in Britain. This total includes wall boxes, free-standing pillar boxes and lamp boxes. Lamp boxes are so called because it was

originally intended that they be affixed to lamp posts though they are now to be seen, for example, attached to telegraph poles or embedded in walls.

With the need for such a large quantity of boxes it is not surprising that the Post Office put their manufacture in the hands of outside contractors. Those to the fore include W. T. Allen and Company of London, Carron Company of Falkirk, Cochrane and Company of Dudley and Andrew Handyside and Company of Derby. With the exception of Allen's, which applies to only lamp and wall boxes, these names will often be found cast around the black-painted bases of pillar boxes.

Quite a number of unusual or rare boxes dating from the mid nineteenth century remain in use and specimens worthy of mention include: in Banbury a fluted pillar box of 1856 but since renovated; in Framlingham two octagonal boxes with vertical apertures, 1856-7; at World's End, Hampshire, a cylindrical stove-like box, 1850s or 1860s; in Liverpool crown-topped boxes peculiar to the city but unfortunately dwindling in numbers, 1863; in Cambridge, Truro and elsewhere hexagonal 'Penfold' boxes, 1860s or 1870s.

One of several hexagonal letter boxes in Cheltenham, Gloucestershire, designed by J. W. Penfold. This box was made by Cochrane, Grove and Company of Dudley and dates from the 1860s or 1870s.

LEFT: *Once a familiar sight to road users, the Automobile Association members' telephone box has now all but disappeared, being replaced by modern pedestal-type telephones. This box stood near Willersley, Hereford and Worcester.*

RIGHT: *Despite its distinct lean, this aging Post Office telephone box shows fewer signs of wear and tear than now do many other boxes of the same type. The box was designed by the architect Sir Giles Gilbert Scott and introduced in 1927. This one dates from the 1930s. Note the reeding and the perforated crowns.*

TELEPHONE BOXES

Telephones came into extensive use in Britain in the 1880s. The first public telephones were put into shops, post offices and railway stations but by 1900 a variety of kiosks had begun to appear on the streets as well. Many were quite attractive but, particularly after the Post Office had taken over the entire telephone system (except Hull), there was a need for a standard design everyone could recognise.

In 1921 kiosk number 1 appeared, cast in concrete and glazed on three sides, including the wooden door. On the roof enamelled boards, bearing the word TELEPHONE, were surmounted by scrolled ironwork. The boxes were well received and examples survive (see page 23) but it was felt that a more attractive design was called for and a design competition was held.

In response Sir Giles Gilbert Scott, the

celebrated architect, designed the first cast iron kiosk (number 2), introduced in 1927. The boxes which survive can be identified by the eighteen glass panels in each side, surmounted by perforated crown ventilators. Probably the most familiar box today is still the 'Jubilee' (number 6) also designed by Scott. Introduced in 1936, it became the first national standard design.

Kingston-upon-Hull is unique in having a telephone system of its own operated independently of British Telecom. The city possesses about four hundred call boxes similar to British Telecom ones except that they are coloured cream and do not bear the royal crown.

At one time the streets of the London Metropolitan Police area were fairly liberally provided with call boxes for emergency use by the general public as well as by the police. Such boxes of precast concrete painted dark blue served as combined telephone boxes and temporary cells, and their roofs each carried a white lamp which could be flashed if it was needed to attract the attention of the local patrol. Virtually all of these boxes were withdrawn in 1969 as police communications became more sophisticated. For a time only one remained operative and this stood beside the A1 road near Bignell's Corner, Hertfordshire.

The City of London has its own police force, which employs a small, pillar-type box with flashable lamp and a telephone available for public use but, because of its size, no cell. Boxes of this type were not exclusive to London and could also be seen in some provincial towns.

The Royal Automobile Club was founded as the Automobile Club in 1897. The Club's first roadside telephone was set up in the Club box at Egham, Surrey, in 1919. Numbers have since grown to a total of about six hundred telephone box or post types.

The Automobile Association was founded in 1905 and introduced its first roadside box in 1911 or 1912. At first boxes were intended for staff use but were subsequently made available to members having the necessary key. Up to the late 1960s the black and yellow AA box with gabled roof was a familiar sight to road users. Then the now common canister unit began to displace the old step-in boxes, which, even if less economical, at least afforded some shelter for the distressed motorist.

ABOVE: *The precast concrete Metropolitan Police public call box which stood beside the A1 road near Bignell's Corner, Hertfordshire. This box was the last of its type left in service.*

RIGHT: *A kiosk number 1 still in use at Bembridge, Isle of Wight, and scheduled in 1986 as a building of historic interest. The door and glazing bars are painted red.*

OPHTHALMIC OP
TELEPHONE
TELEPHONE

The Matlock cable tramway, the steepest cable-operated road tramway in Britain, ceased running in 1927. However, this timber-constructed tram passenger shelter survives in Matlock, Derbyshire.

A sight to delight the heart of the street furniture enthusiast. This fine iron passenger shelter in Northampton was made by D. Rowell and Company of London and is attractively painted in red, white and blue.

SHELTERS

Passenger shelters have played a significant, if now diminishing, role in the journeyings of a large proportion of the travelling public. Nevertheless, despite the prominence of shelters in the average townscape, their merits often go unnoticed and unappreciated.

In the stagecoach era those intending to travel any distance usually waited for their transport in or by a relatively comfortable inn. Those less fortunate were sometimes obliged to stand at the roadside in whatever weather conditions prevailed until their coach arrived. Travelling comfort may have improved in more recent times but waiting conditions have not always made any progress at all!

Horse buses and horse trams were introduced in Britain in 1829 and 1860 respectively. Electric trams and motor buses followed in the 1880s and 1890s. It is uncertain when and where the first passenger shelter was set up although shelters would probably have been erected soon after regular services became established.

In contrast to many current urban types which are of comparatively light metal construction, early shelters tended to be somewhat heavily built with much use being made of cast iron, timber and glass. Losses due to wartime bombing, and extensive scrappings since to make way for modern replacements, have caused the disappearance of many fine old specimens. Although in danger of extinction, good examples do still exist here and there and are worth seeking and studying.

If not always serving any useful purpose apart from a purely visual one, the ornamentation of a shelter at least contributed to the grace, or ugliness, of what might otherwise have been merely another undistinguished roadside object. In some cases successive layers of paint have unfortunately blurred the finer details of cast iron work and even obliterated the name, and possibly the address, of the makers.

Not only shelters can prove interesting but sometimes the seating also. While this frequently consists merely of a wooden bench suffering from vandalism, one may sometimes encounter a fascinating cast iron seat or a redundant bench acquired from a local railway station or elsewhere.

Though their numbers are declining, London still possesses a few aging cabmen's shelters, notably in the vicinity of the Victoria Embankment and in Leicester Square. These shelters originated in the horse-cab days of Queen Victoria when benefactors helped to provide suitable places of rest for drivers. Horse-drawn cabs were ultimately displaced from the streets of London in the early years of the present century but the shelters were retained for continuing use by taxicab drivers.

With some variations in size, cabmen's shelters conform, more or less, to a basic style, the distinctive features of which include timber construction, green paintwork, opaque glass windows and a louvred ventilation cote on a tiled or shingled roof.

Lean-to public urinal, Star Yard, Holborn, London.

ABOVE: *The very impressive silver-painted iron tram passenger shelter latterly used by bus passengers in Cosham, Hampshire. This shelter, like the one shown on page 25, was made by D. Rowell and Company of London.*

BELOW: *The timber-constructed shelter in the village of Adlestrop, Gloucestershire, contains an erstwhile Great Western Railway station bench and station nameboard acquired from the now closed local halt.*

A verbose weight restriction sign at the approach to the canal bridge at Startop's End, Buckinghamshire.

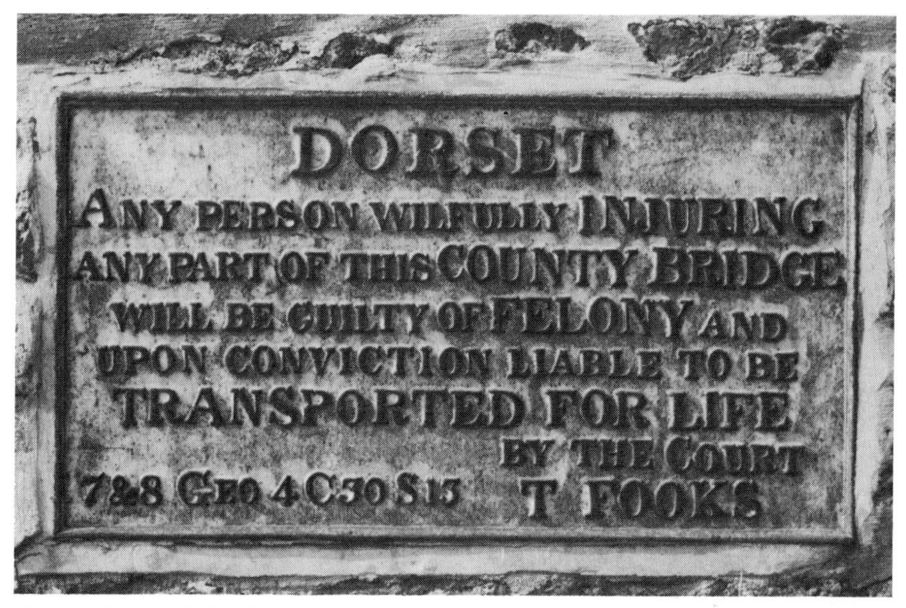

An iron plate attached to the parapet of a bridge over the river Lydden near Kingstag, Dorset. Dating from the reign of George IV and typical of the county of Dorset, these plates warn of the penalty of transportation for life.

TRAFFIC SIGNS AND SIGNALS

In contrast to their present-day proliferation, traffic signs in the pioneer days of motoring were, not unnaturally, few and far between. Early in the twentieth century the erection of what signs there then were was largely in the hands of the Automobile Association, local motoring clubs and cycling clubs. Such signs are now almost extinct. Some remain for the finding but in the interests of their licit preservation it would be unwise to divulge precise locations.

Whereas current practice favours the use of reflectively coated or internally illuminated signs their predecessors were stove-enamelled or simply painted and, in some cases, studded with clear or red glass reflectors. The principal manufacturers of past and present road signs include The Forest City Signs Limited, Franco-Signs Limited and the Royal Label Factory.

Of all the different kinds of hazard confronting road users over the years bridges have given rise to possibly the greatest number and variety of related signs. These have included signs warning of hump, low, narrow and weak bridges.

Dorset is renowned for the iron signs attached to the parapets of several of its river bridges. Dating from the reign of George IV, they warn of the dire possibility of transportation for anyone found guilty of maliciously damaging a bridge.

Sixty or so years later the coming of traction engines and other heavy vehicles led to the putting up nationally of weight-restriction signs beside roads leading to many canal, railway and river bridges. Frequently diamond in shape, such signs have become rarer although they are still to be seen at the approaches to lightly constructed canal bridges.

More recent, yet rare not because of age but because minor suspension bridges are few, were the signs requesting marching columns to break step on crossing for fear that not to do so might have created vibrations harmful to the bridge.

The City of Westminster had what may be regarded as the first traffic signal in Britain. Set up in 1868, professedly to help Members of Parliament making their way to the House, this signal had semaphore arms, was illuminated by gas and operated by hand. Unfortunately its working life was brief for it suffered a gas explosion in the following year and was dismantled in 1872. The signal's manufacturers, Saxby and Farmer Limited, were later absorbed into the Westinghouse Brake and Saxby Signal Company Limited, one of the leading makers of electric signals and installers in 1927 of the first signals in Piccadilly Circus. The Forest City Signs Limited were also pioneers in the field, having first imported signals from America in 1928 and then from the late 1930s manufactured them in Britain.

The Forest City signals are of interest in that in addition to the word 'Stop' on the red aspects they also displayed the word 'Go' on the green. Both words have been dispensed with on the larger signals more recently produced by GEC-Elliott Traffic Automation Limited.

LEFT: *Traffic sign with glass reflectors warning of a multiple junction ahead, at Salcombe, Devon.*

NEAR RIGHT: *An extra-tall weight restriction sign in Buxton, Derbyshire. Note the surmounting red disc, now obsolete but typical of road traffic warning signs in the 1930s.*

FAR RIGHT: *A now rare traffic signal in Northampton. This signal was made by The Forest City Signs Ltd of Altrincham and is noteworthy for having the word 'Go' on the green aspect.*

FURTHER READING

Aaron, Henry. *Pillar to Post: Looking at Street Furniture*. Frederick Warne, 1982.

Emmerson, Andrew. *Old Telephones*. Shire, 1986; reprinted 1990.

Farrugia, Jean Young. *The Letter Box: A History of Post Office Pillar and Wall Boxes*. Centaur Press, 1969.

Fearn, Jacqueline. *Cast Iron*. Shire, 1990.

Garvey, Jude. *A Guide to the Transport Museums of Great Britain*. Pelham Books, 1982.

Richardson, John. *The Local Historian's Encyclopaedia*. Historical Publications, 1974.

Robinson, Martin. *Old Letter Boxes*. Shire, 1987; reprinted 1992.

PLACES TO VISIT

Intending visitors are advised to check times of opening before making a special journey.

Beamish: The North of England Open Air Museum, Beamish, Stanley, County Durham DH9 0RG. Telephone: 0207 231811.

Blists Hill Open Air Museum, Legges Way, Madeley, Telford, Shropshire TF7 5DU. Telephone: 0952 586063, 583003 or 586309.

East Anglia Transport Museum, Chapel Road, Carlton Colville, Lowestoft, Suffolk NR33 8BL. Telephone: 0502 518459.

National Tramway Museum, Crich, Matlock, Derbyshire DE4 5DP. Telephone: 0773 852565.

Salford Museum and Art Gallery, Peel Park, The Crescent, Salford, Lancashire M5 4WU. Telephone: 061-736 2649.

Ulster American Folk Park, Camphill, Omagh, County Tyrone, Northern Ireland BT78 5QY. Telephone: 0662 243292 or 243293.

Street orderly bin, Blackfriars Bridge, London. Note the sliding top, hinged doors, litter baskets and grit or sand hole.